Blackwell's Little Learning Library

KU-350-319

ELECTRICITY

BASIL BLACKWELL OXFORD

Look up at the ceiling.

Is there an electric light there?

How do you make it light up?

Why do you think this happens?

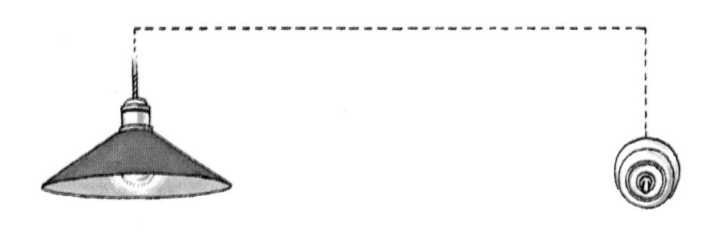

Think of all the other things
    which work by electricity.

Have you ever asked anyone
    where electricity comes from?

Let us find out something about it.

The building in the distance
is a power station.

The wire cables between the pylons
carry electricity from it.

Not all electricity comes
   along cables hanging from pylons.

Some comes in cables underground.

But all our electricity is made
   at power stations.

Huge machines make it,
   and we call it a "current".

It runs along cables and wires,
   though we cannot see it.

Electricity can KILL YOU
   if you touch any bare wires.

That is why wires are covered,
   or kept away from us.

These generators make electricity
at the power station.

They may be driven by steam,
or by water, or by atomic power.

Electricity from a power station
   comes right to our homes.

There we use it for many things.

We must pay for it, of course,
   so we have a meter.

Here is one kind.

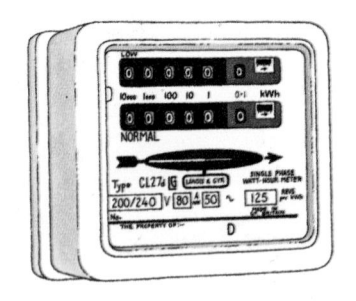

The meter measures
   how much electricity we use.

Electric lights do not use
very much current.

Most of them are just thin wires
made very hot.

Here are some different lamps.

Have you seen the wire
inside a light bulb?

It takes much more current
to make electric fires hot.

The hot parts are called elements.

Here are two kinds of fire.

You can see the elements of one,
but the other sends out warm air.

Here are two
other kinds
of "fire".

The kettle's element boils water.

The iron's element makes it hot.

This cooker
has several
elements.

How many
can you see
on the top?

Where are
the others?

A cooker uses a lot of current.

Electricity will also drive motors.

What electric machines do you know?

There is a motor
    in a hair drier.

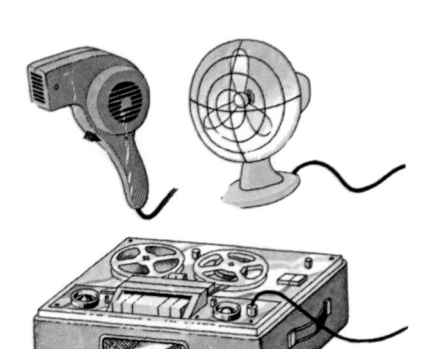

There is one
    in a fan.

There is one
    in a
    tape recorder.

There is one
    in a
    dentist's drill.

There are electric motors in some typewriters, projectors, razors, mixers, tin-openers, record-players, and even some for tooth-brushes!

Here are two more electric motors.

Bigger electric motors are used
on some railways.

Here is one kind of giant engine for
pulling trains.

It takes current for its motors
from the wire up above.

Some trains take their current
from another rail on the ground.

Their engines are underneath
some of the coaches.

Underground trains in London
run in this way.

Many more electric motors
   are used in factories.

Others are used on farms,
   even to milk cows.

Try to find out about electricity
   used in hospitals.

There are very many more things
 which work from electricity.

Here are some.

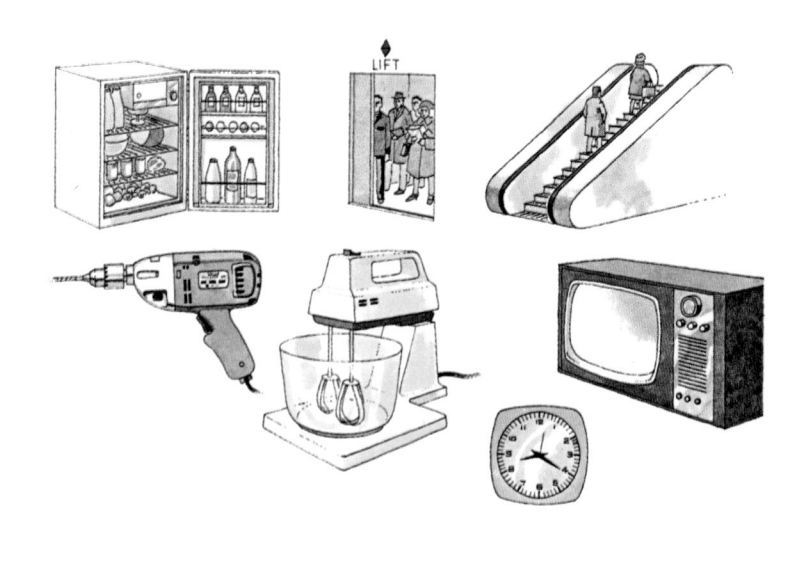

Write down some others.

Do you know the answers?

Where is electricity made?

What do we call the machines
   which make the current?

How does electricity come to us?

Why must we not touch bare wires
   carrying current?

How do we know how much current
   we use at home?

How do Underground trains work?

How can electricity boil water?

How can it help us to eat?